My first HERBARIUM - A notebook for collecting and identifying plants
© 2019 by Funky Banana Notebooks. All rights reserved. No part of this book may be used or reproduced in any manner whatsoever without written permission except in the case of brief quotations embodied in critical articles and reviews.
1. Edition: 2019

You can find a How to Use with infos and tips on the last page of this book.

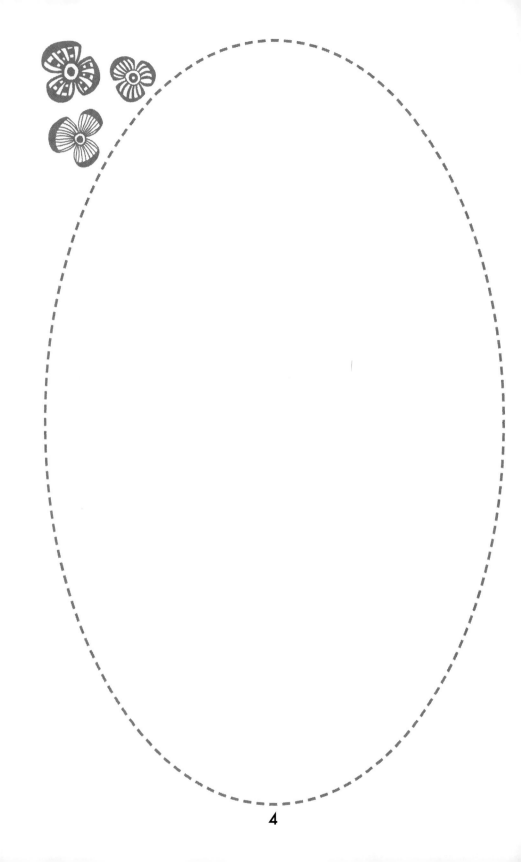

Date: ....

Common Name: ....

Scientific Name: ....

Location: .... Size: ....

Leaves: .... Flowers: ....

Fruits: .... Roots: ....

Stem: .... Habitat: ....

Effect & Usage: ....

Date: ....

Common Name: ....

Scientific Name: ....

Location: .... Size: ....

Leaves: .... Flowers: ....

Fruits: .... Roots: ....

Stem: .... Habitat: ....

Effect & Usage: ....

Date: ....

Common Name: ....

Scientific Name: ....

Location: .... Size: ....

Leaves: .... Flowers: ....

Fruits: .... Roots: ....

Stem: .... Habitat: ....

Effect & Usage: ....

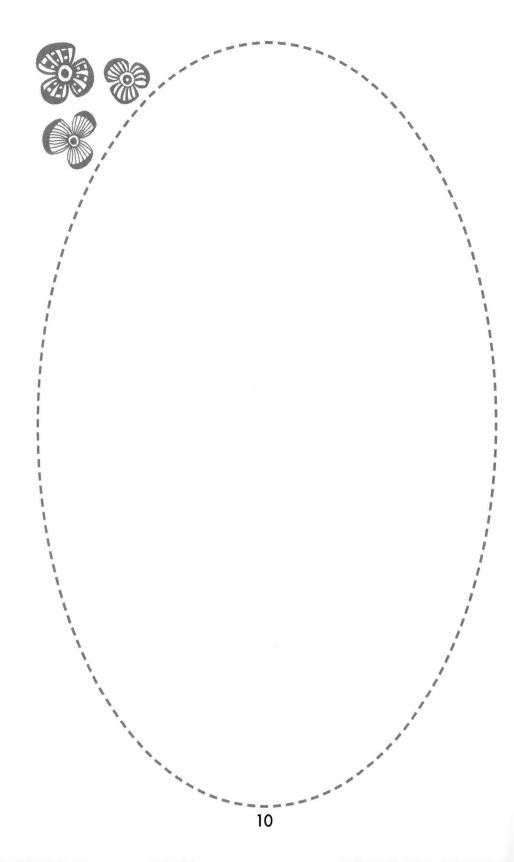

Date: ....

Common Name: ....

Scientific Name: ....

Location: .... Size: ....

Leaves: .... Flowers: ....

Fruits: .... Roots: ....

Stem: .... Habitat: ....

Effect & Usage: ....

Date: ....

Common Name: ....

Scientific Name: ....

Location: .... Size: ....

Leaves: .... Flowers: ....

Fruits: .... Roots: ....

Stem: .... Habitat: ....

Effect & Usage: ....

Date: ....

Common Name: ....

Scientific Name: ....

Location: .... Size: ....

Leaves: .... Flowers: ....

Fruits: .... Roots: ....

Stem: .... Habitat: ....

Effect & Usage: ....

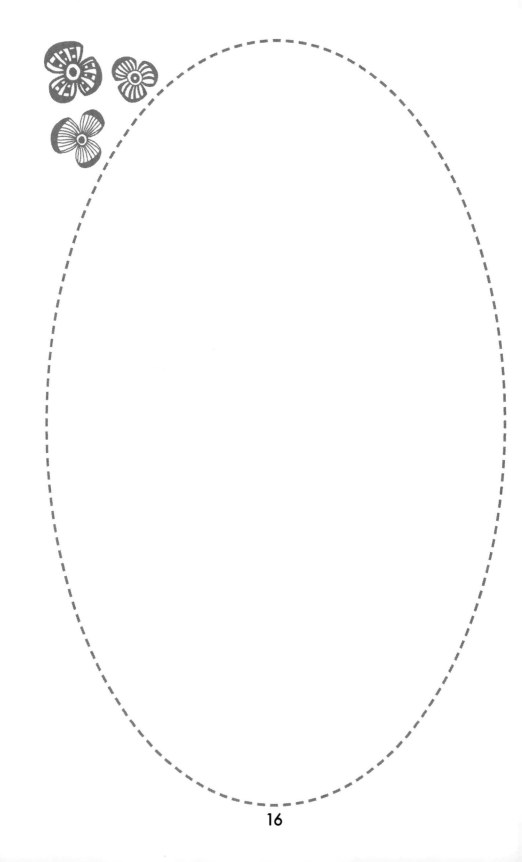

Date: ....

Common Name: ....

Scientific Name: ....

Location: .... Size: ....

Leaves: .... Flowers: ....

Fruits: .... Roots: ....

Stem: .... Habitat: ....

Effect & Usage: ....

Date: ....

Common Name: ....

Scientific Name: ....

Location: .... Size: ....

Leaves: .... Flowers: ....

Fruits: .... Roots: ....

Stem: .... Habitat: ....

Effect & Usage: ....

Date: ....

Common Name: ....

Scientific Name: ....

Location: .... Size: ....

Leaves: .... Flowers: ....

Fruits: .... Roots: ....

Stem: .... Habitat: ....

Effect & Usage: ....

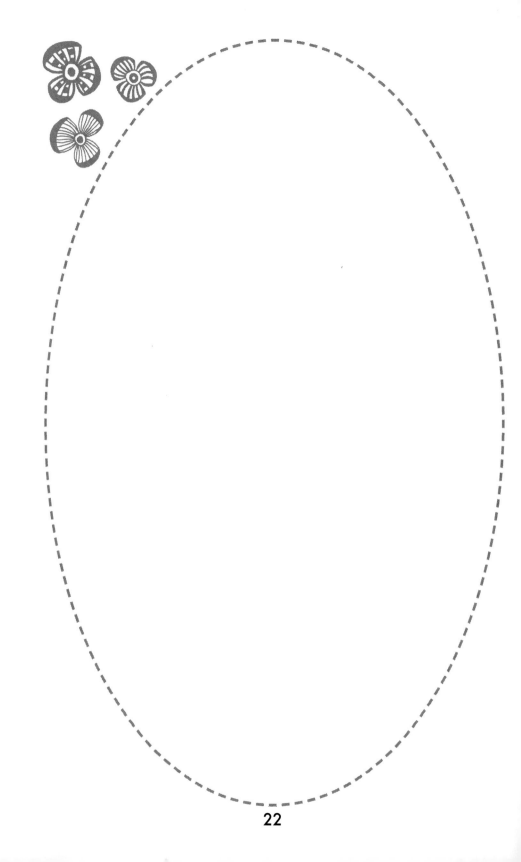

Date: ....

Common Name: ....

Scientific Name: ....

Location: .... Size: ....

Leaves: .... Flowers: ....

Fruits: .... Roots: ....

Stem: .... Habitat: ....

Effect & Usage: ....

23

Date: ....

Common Name: ....

Scientific Name: ....

Location: .... Size: ....

Leaves: .... Flowers: ....

Fruits: .... Roots: ....

Stem: .... Habitat: ....

Effect & Usage: ....

25

Date: ....

Common Name: ....

Scientific Name: ....

Location: .... Size: ....

Leaves: .... Flowers: ....

Fruits: .... Roots: ....

Stem: .... Habitat: ....

Effect & Usage: ....

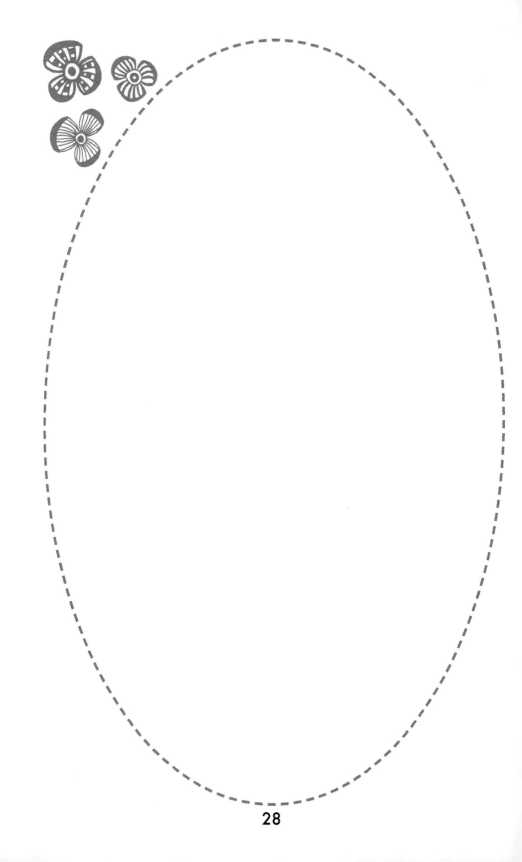

Date: ....

Common Name: ....

Scientific Name: ....

Location: .... Size: ....

Leaves: .... Flowers: ....

Fruits: .... Roots: ....

Stem: .... Habitat: ....

Effect & Usage: ....

Date: ....

Common Name: ....

Scientific Name: ....

Location: .... Size: ....

Leaves: .... Flowers: ....

Fruits: .... Roots: ....

Stem: .... Habitat: ....

Effect & Usage: ....

Date: ....

Common Name: ....

Scientific Name: ....

Location: .... Size: ....

Leaves: .... Flowers: ....

Fruits: .... Roots: ....

Stem: .... Habitat: ....

Effect & Usage: ....

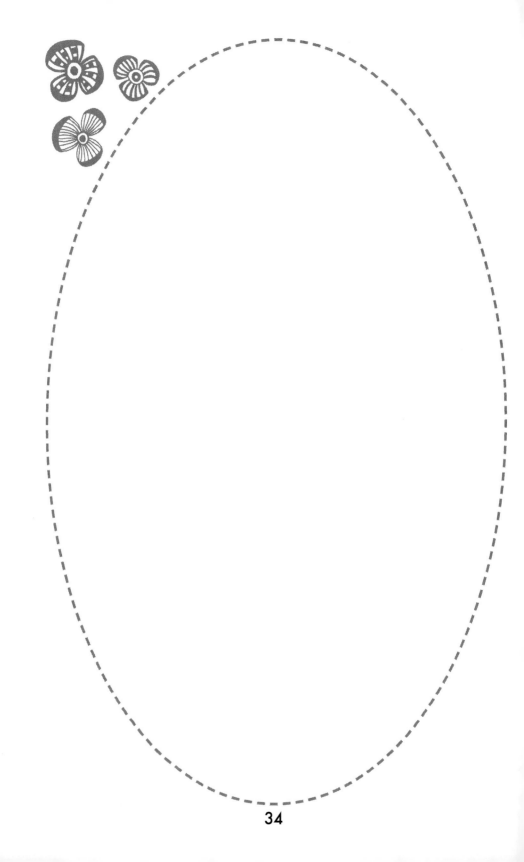

Date: ....

Common Name: ....

Scientific Name: ....

Location: .... Size: ....

Leaves: .... Flowers: ....

Fruits: .... Roots: ....

Stem: .... Habitat: ....

Effect & Usage: ....

Date: ....

Common Name: ....

Scientific Name: ....

Location: .... Size: ....

Leaves: .... Flowers: ....

Fruits: .... Roots: ....

Stem: .... Habitat: ....

Effect & Usage: ....

37

Date: ....

Common Name: ....

Scientific Name: ....

Location: .... Size: ....

Leaves: .... Flowers: ....

Fruits: .... Roots: ....

Stem: .... Habitat: ....

Effect & Usage: ....

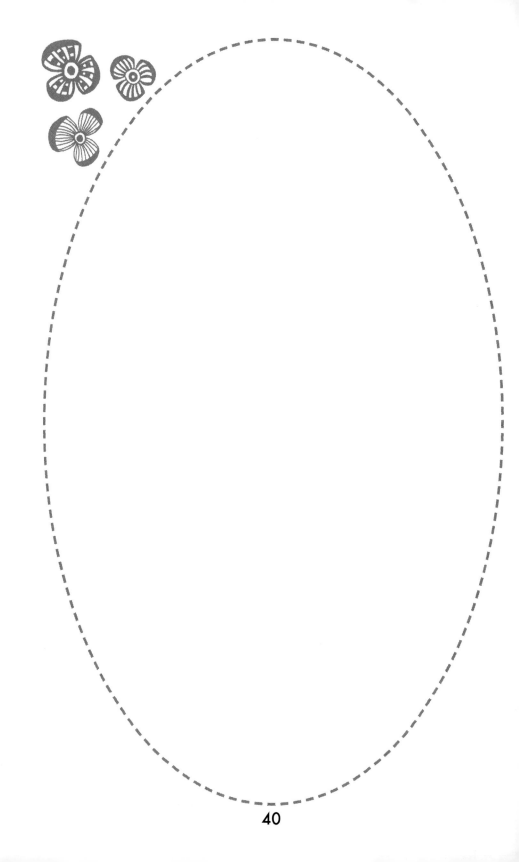

Date: ....

Common Name: ....

Scientific Name: ....

Location: .... Size: ....

Leaves: .... Flowers: ....

Fruits: .... Roots: ....

Stem: .... Habitat: ....

Effect & Usage: ....

Date: ....

Common Name: ....

Scientific Name: ....

Location: .... Size: ....

Leaves: .... Flowers: ....

Fruits: .... Roots: ....

Stem: .... Habitat: ....

Effect & Usage: ....

Date: ....

Common Name: ....

Scientific Name: ....

Location: .... Size: ....

Leaves: .... Flowers: ....

Fruits: .... Roots: ....

Stem: .... Habitat: ....

Effect & Usage: ....

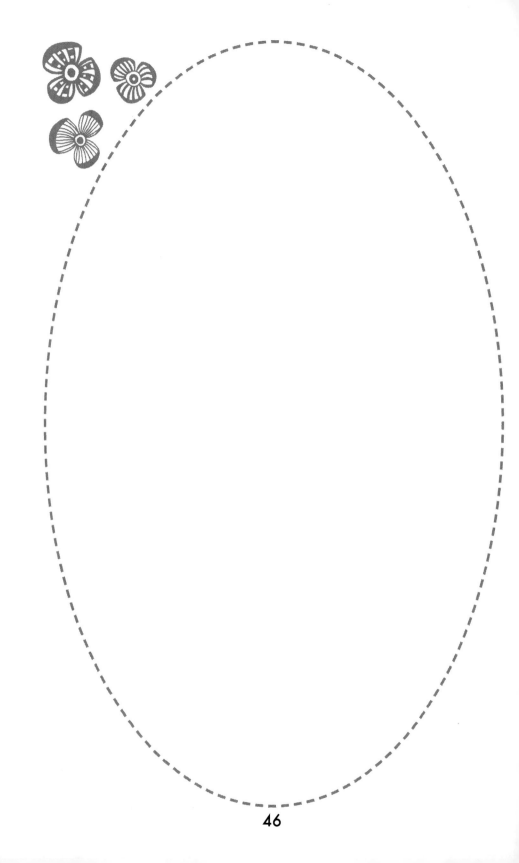

Date: ....

Common Name: ....

Scientific Name: ....

Location: .... Size: ....

Leaves: .... Flowers: ....

Fruits: .... Roots: ....

Stem: .... Habitat: ....

Effect & Usage: ....

Date: ....

Common Name: ....

Scientific Name: ....

Location: .... Size: ....

Leaves: .... Flowers: ....

Fruits: .... Roots: ....

Stem: .... Habitat: ....

Effect & Usage: ....

49

Date: ....

Common Name: ....

Scientific Name: ....

Location: .... Size: ....

Leaves: .... Flowers: ....

Fruits: .... Roots: ....

Stem: .... Habitat: ....

Effect & Usage: ....

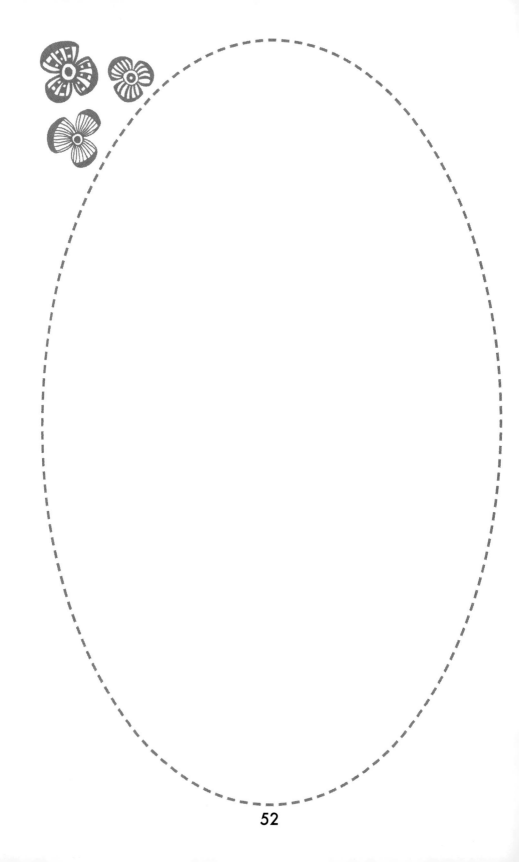

Date: ....

Common Name: ....

Scientific Name: ....

Location: .... Size: ....

Leaves: .... Flowers: ....

Fruits: .... Roots: ....

Stem: .... Habitat: ....

Effect & Usage: ....

Date: ....

Common Name: ....

Scientific Name: ....

Location: .... Size: ....

Leaves: .... Flowers: ....

Fruits: .... Roots: ....

Stem: .... Habitat: ....

Effect & Usage: ....

Date: ....

Common Name: ....

Scientific Name: ....

Location: .... Size: ....

Leaves: .... Flowers: ....

Fruits: .... Roots: ....

Stem: .... Habitat: ....

Effect & Usage: ....

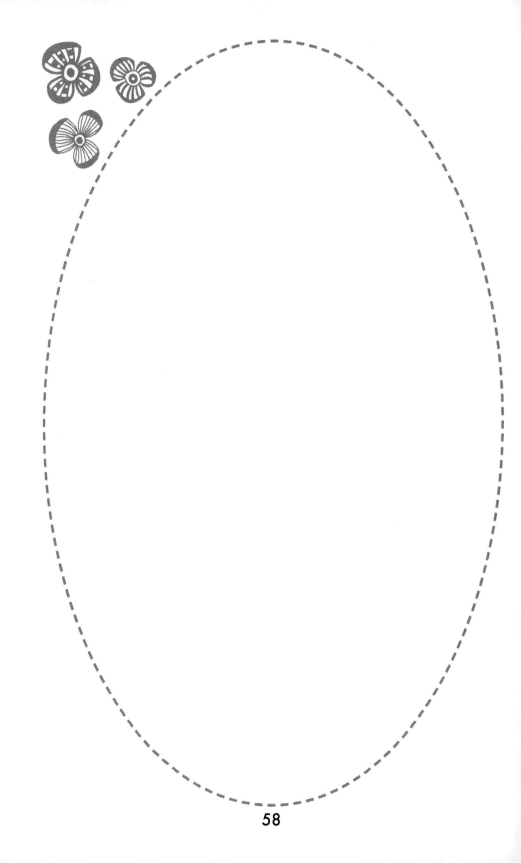

Date: ....

Common Name: ....

Scientific Name: ....

Location: .... Size: ....

Leaves: .... Flowers: ....

Fruits: .... Roots: ....

Stem: .... Habitat: ....

Effect & Usage: ....

Date: ....

Common Name: ....
Scientific Name: ....
Location: .... Size: ....
Leaves: .... Flowers: ....
Fruits: .... Roots: ....
Stem: .... Habitat: ....
Effect & Usage: ....

Date: ....

Common Name: ....

Scientific Name: ....

Location: .... Size: ....

Leaves: .... Flowers: ....

Fruits: .... Roots: ....

Stem: .... Habitat: ....

Effect & Usage: ....

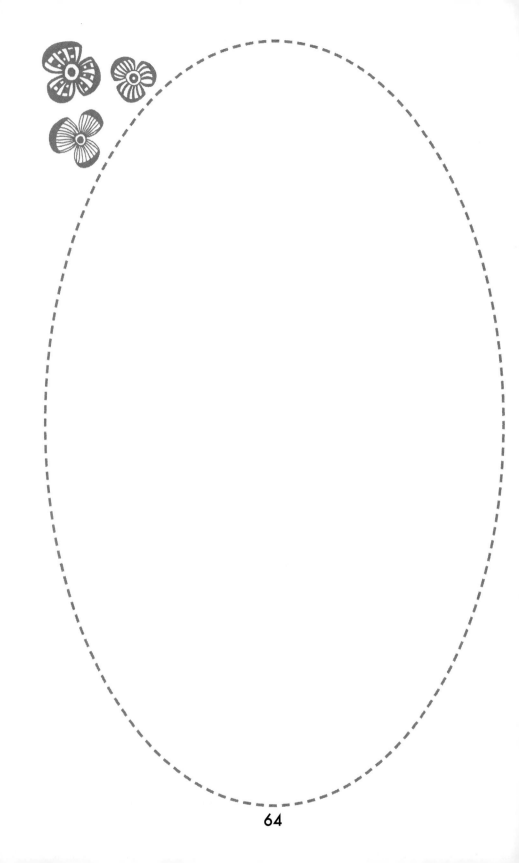

Date: ....

Common Name: ....

Scientific Name: ....

Location: .... Size: ....

Leaves: .... Flowers: ....

Fruits: .... Roots: ....

Stem: .... Habitat: ....

Effect & Usage: ....

Date: ....

Common Name: ....

Scientific Name: ....

Location: .... Size: ....

Leaves: .... Flowers: ....

Fruits: .... Roots: ....

Stem: .... Habitat: ....

Effect & Usage: ....

Date: ....

Common Name: ....

Scientific Name: ....

Location: .... Size: ....

Leaves: .... Flowers: ....

Fruits: .... Roots: ....

Stem: .... Habitat: ....

Effect & Usage: ....

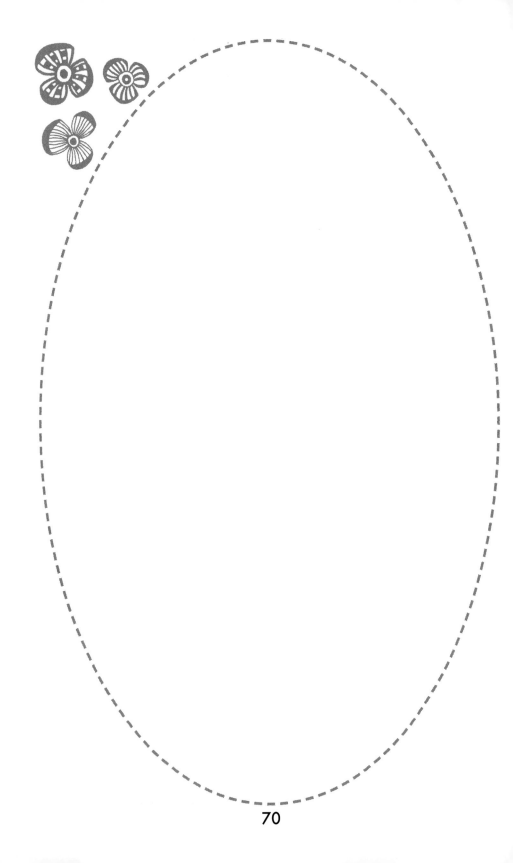

Date: ....

Common Name: ....

Scientific Name: ....

Location: .... Size: ....

Leaves: .... Flowers: ....

Fruits: .... Roots: ....

Stem: .... Habitat: ....

Effect & Usage: ....

71

Date: ....

Common Name: ....

Scientific Name: ....

Location: .... Size: ....

Leaves: .... Flowers: ....

Fruits: .... Roots: ....

Stem: .... Habitat: ....

Effect & Usage: ....

Date: ....

Common Name: ....

Scientific Name: ....

Location: .... Size: ....

Leaves: .... Flowers: ....

Fruits: .... Roots: ....

Stem: .... Habitat: ....

Effect & Usage: ....

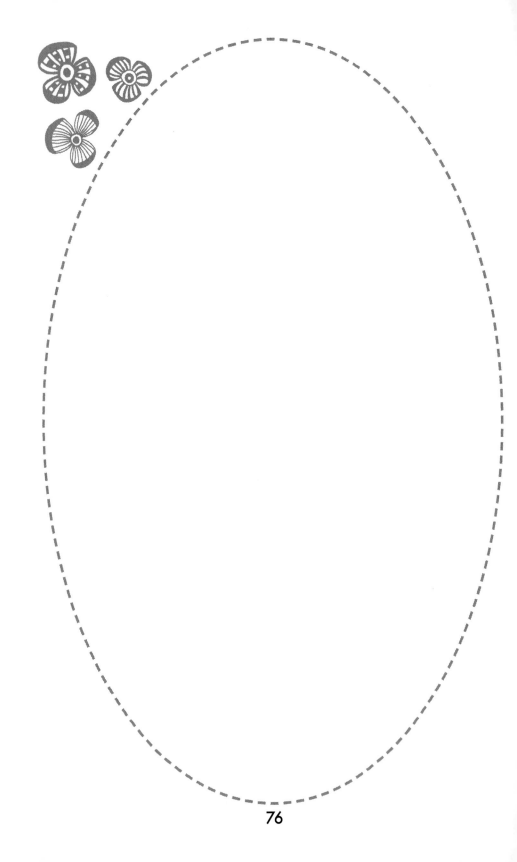

Date: ....

Common Name: ....

Scientific Name: ....

Location: .... Size: ....

Leaves: .... Flowers: ....

Fruits: .... Roots: ....

Stem: .... Habitat: ....

Effect & Usage: ....

Date: ....

Common Name: ....

Scientific Name: ....

Location: .... Size: ....

Leaves: .... Flowers: ....

Fruits: .... Roots: ....

Stem: .... Habitat: ....

Effect & Usage: ....

Date: ....

Common Name: ....

Scientific Name: ....

Location: .... Size: ....

Leaves: .... Flowers: ....

Fruits: .... Roots: ....

Stem: .... Habitat: ....

Effect & Usage: ....

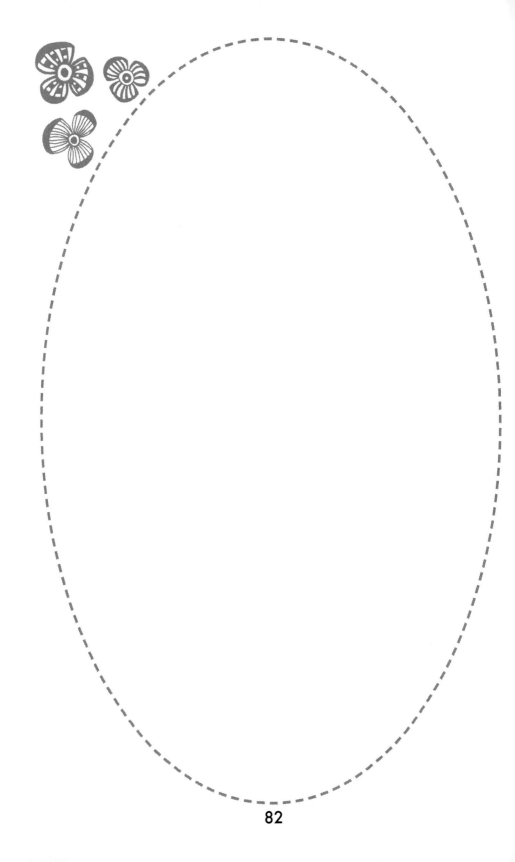

Date: ....

Common Name: ....

Scientific Name: ....

Location: .... Size: ....

Leaves: .... Flowers: ....

Fruits: .... Roots: ....

Stem: .... Habitat: ....

Effect & Usage: ....

Date: ....

Common Name: ....

Scientific Name: ....

Location: .... Size: ....

Leaves: .... Flowers: ....

Fruits: .... Roots: ....

Stem: .... Habitat: ....

Effect & Usage: ....

Date: ....

Common Name: ....

Scientific Name: ....

Location: .... Size: ....

Leaves: .... Flowers: ....

Fruits: .... Roots: ....

Stem: .... Habitat: ....

Effect & Usage: ....

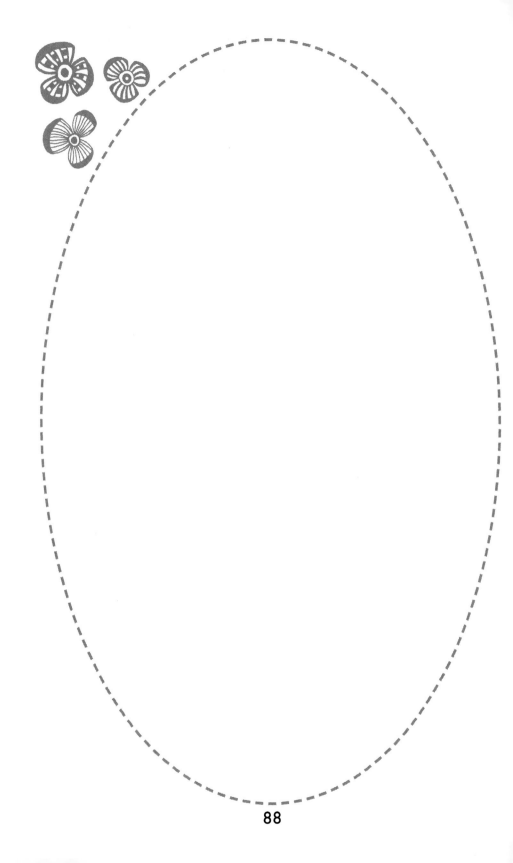

Date: ....

Common Name: ....

Scientific Name: ....

Location: .... Size: ....

Leaves: .... Flowers: ....

Fruits: .... Roots: ....

Stem: .... Habitat: ....

Effect & Usage: ....

Date: ....

Common Name: ....

Scientific Name: ....

Location: .... Size: ....

Leaves: .... Flowers: ....

Fruits: .... Roots: ....

Stem: .... Habitat: ....

Effect & Usage: ....

Date: ....

Common Name: ....

Scientific Name: ....

Location: .... Size: ....

Leaves: .... Flowers: ....

Fruits: .... Roots: ....

Stem: .... Habitat: ....

Effect & Usage: ....

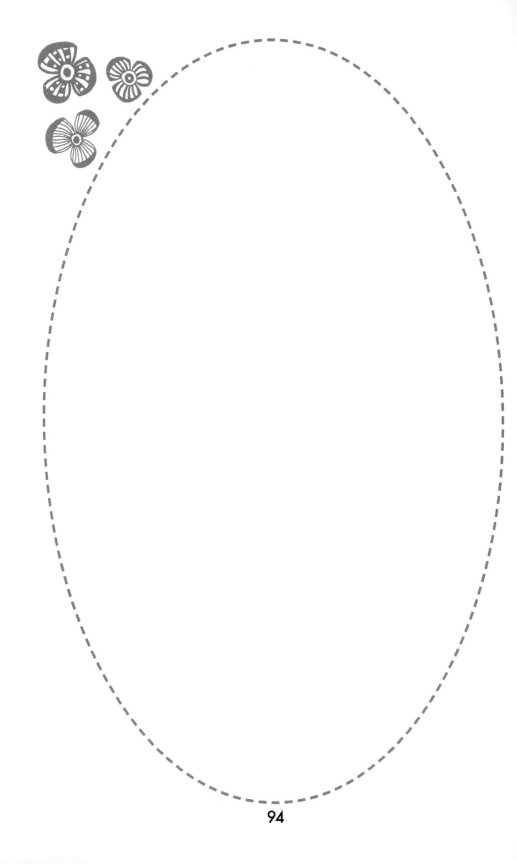

Date: ....

Common Name: ....

Scientific Name: ....

Location: .... Size: ....

Leaves: .... Flowers: ....

Fruits: .... Roots: ....

Stem: .... Habitat: ....

Effect & Usage: ....

Date: ....

Common Name: ....

Scientific Name: ....

Location: .... Size: ....

Leaves: .... Flowers: ....

Fruits: .... Roots: ....

Stem: .... Habitat: ....

Effect & Usage: ....

Date: ....

Common Name: ....

Scientific Name: ....

Location: .... Size: ....

Leaves: .... Flowers: ....

Fruits: .... Roots: ....

Stem: .... Habitat: ....

Effect & Usage: ....

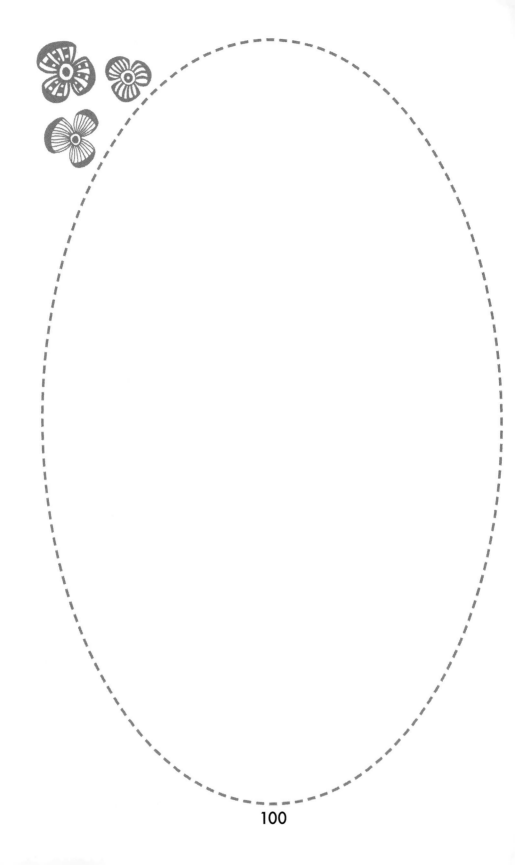

Date: ....

Common Name: ....

Scientific Name: ....

Location: .... Size: ....

Leaves: .... Flowers: ....

Fruits: .... Roots: ....

Stem: .... Habitat: ....

Effect & Usage: ....

Date: ....

Common Name: ....
Scientific Name: ....
Location: .... Size: ....
Leaves: .... Flowers: ....
Fruits: .... Roots: ....
Stem: .... Habitat: ....
Effect & Usage: ....

103

Date: ....

Common Name: ....

Scientific Name: ....

Location: .... Size: ....

Leaves: .... Flowers: ....

Fruits: .... Roots: ....

Stem: .... Habitat: ....

Effect & Usage: ....

105

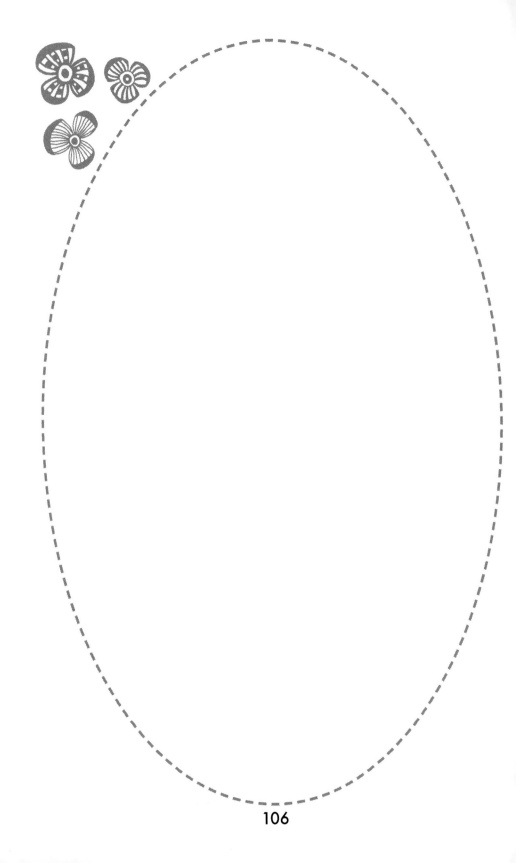

Date: ....

Common Name: ....

Scientific Name: ....

Location: .... Size: ....

Leaves: .... Flowers: ....

Fruits: .... Roots: ....

Stem: .... Habitat: ....

Effect & Usage: ....

Date: ....

Common Name: ....

Scientific Name: ....

Location: .... Size: ....

Leaves: .... Flowers: ....

Fruits: .... Roots: ....

Stem: .... Habitat: ....

Effect & Usage: ....

Date: ....

Common Name: ....

Scientific Name: ....

Location: .... Size: ....

Leaves: .... Flowers: ....

Fruits: .... Roots: ....

Stem: .... Habitat: ....

Effect & Usage: ....

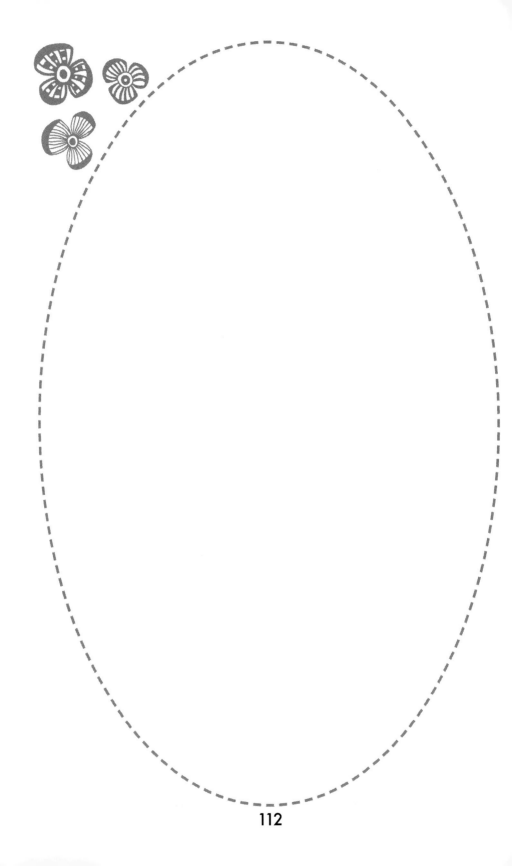

Date: ....

Common Name: ....

Scientific Name: ....

Location: .... Size: ....

Leaves: .... Flowers: ....

Fruits: .... Roots: ....

Stem: .... Habitat: ....

Effect & Usage: ....

Date: ....

Common Name: ....

Scientific Name: ....

Location: .... Size: ....

Leaves: .... Flowers: ....

Fruits: .... Roots: ....

Stem: .... Habitat: ....

Effect & Usage: ....

Date: ....

Common Name: ....
Scientific Name: ....
Location: .... Size: ....
Leaves: .... Flowers: ....
Fruits: .... Roots: ....
Stem: .... Habitat: ....
Effect & Usage: ....

117

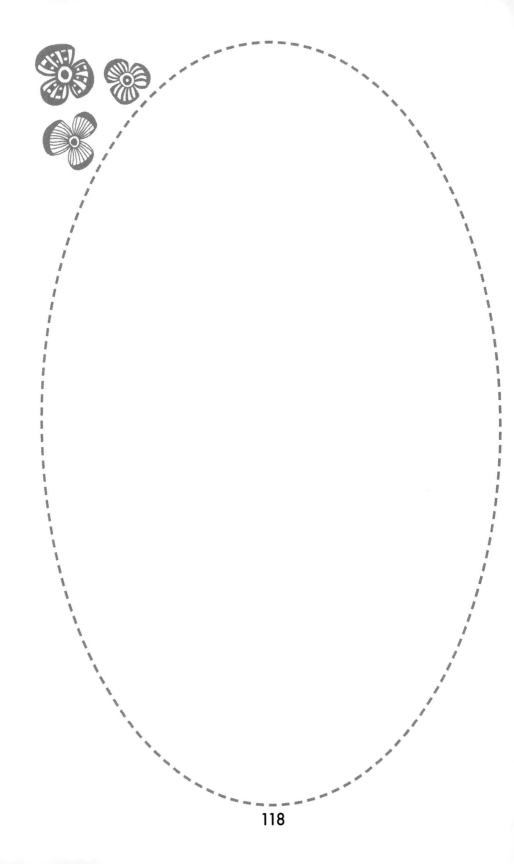

Date: ....

Common Name: ....

Scientific Name: ....

Location: .... Size: ....

Leaves: .... Flowers: ....

Fruits: .... Roots: ....

Stem: .... Habitat: ....

Effect & Usage: ....

Date: ....

Common Name: ....

Scientific Name: ....

Location: .... Size: ....

Leaves: .... Flowers: ....

Fruits: .... Roots: ....

Stem: .... Habitat: ....

Effect & Usage: ....

Date: ....

Common Name: ....

Scientific Name: ....

Location: .... Size: ....

Leaves: .... Flowers: ....

Fruits: .... Roots: ....

Stem: .... Habitat: ....

Effect & Usage: ....

How to use this book

Collect plants, flowers, herbs, whatever you like. However, please be sure and inform yourself so that you only collect plants you're able to identify - it's at your own risk and best to ask a person with botany knowledge for advice. **Caution: Avoid collecting poisonous plants in any case!** When in doubt, stay away from the plant. The author of this book is not responsible for possible injury or damage to your person collecting dangerous and/or poisonous plants. Stay away from the ones that are under conservation and or protection, too. Always collect wisely and with care to not destroy the habitat.

To press plants, you must dry them out as quickly as possible to prevent browning. Put the freshly collected items between two sheets of paper and put them in the heaviest book you can find. The moisture being absorbed might cause damage, so use a book you don't mind to get stained. Use more books or other heavy items to weigh down the book once it's closed. Wait until the flowers and leaves are completely dry, this might take up to two weeks.

Once all your plants and herbs are dry, you're ready to fill your Herbarium.
Glue or tape in the pressed plants to the empty area on the left of each double page. It looks beautiful to arrange several parts of a plant, like flowers and leaves together or one or more plants as a whole. Be careful, dried flowers are very delicate. You can add notes or sketches around your plant, too.
Fill in the information box on the right side of the double page. Here you will also find additional free space to use to your liking. Have fun and get creative!

Printed in Great Britain
by Amazon